Miracles in the Midst of the Storm

By: **Michelle Spicely**

COPYRIGHT © 2024

All rights reserved. No part of this publication may be reproduced, stored in a retrieval system, or transmitted in any form or by any means—electronic, mechanical, photocopy, or any other—except for brief quotations in printed reviews without the prior written permission of the publisher.

Published by: Book Publish Pro

DEDICATION

I dedicate this book to my husband, Donald, of 33 yrs. Who has been more than I ever could have dreamed of in a husband? You are my King and I love you more than you will ever know. You have lived through most of these trials with me. Experienced every miracle by my side. Your compassion, protection, and love has never failed. You are my gift from God.

To my children, David and Joshua, and my step daughter Courtney. I am so proud of the men and woman you have become. Your strength and tenacity is commendable as you strive for your dream. I love all of you so much. Always remember there is no weapon formed that you can't overcome through Christ Jesus. Let my life be a witness to that. You are cut from the same cloth. Let it bind you together for you never can be truly separated.

Donald

David

Courtney

Josh

Table of Contents

Chapter One 1

Chapter Two 7

Chapter Three 14

Chapter Four 16

Chapter Five 20

Chapter Six 24

Chapter Seven 27

Chapter Eight 32

Chapter Nine 36

Chapter Ten 40

Chapter Eleven 44

Chapter Twelve 49

Lessons from My Life 53

Chapter One

I am the youngest of three children, and my family has always been a fundamental part of who I am. My closest brother is two years older, and my other brother is 16 years older than I am.

My oldest son, David, was a gifted child. He started playing drums at the age of two. He now also plays the keyboards, guitar, and percussion instruments. All are predominantly self-taught. He is good at whatever he puts his mind to do. I sat and watched him build a table in front of my eyes. He continues to amaze me whenever I am in his presence. He works at a mega-church where he's in the youth ministry and is studying to be an elder.

He has a lovely wife who is very giving and is constantly concerned about my wellbeing. She gave me three adorable grandchildren who brighten my world whenever I'm around them.

My youngest son, Josh has a Bachelor's Degree in Sociology and a Master's Degree in Education. He is also a football coach; his true passion. The young adults he has worked with adore and look up to him. He often talks to me when I'm down and has seen me through a lot of difficult times. His gift of listening and his caring nature is commendable and is truly a gift from God.

He is engaged to be married to a wonderful young lady who charms everyone she meets. She is very soft-spoken, but don't let that fool you. She is in law school.

I have a daughter through marriage, Courtney who I couldn't love more if she was my very own. I always wanted to be a nurse and my health prevented me from accomplishing that dream. She just graduated and is now an RN. She fast tracked the nursing program while being married, raising two kids, and working a full-time job. No easy feat. So proud of her!

My father, a stern yet playful man, often engaged us in his quirky humor. One of his favorite jokes was the classic "pull my finger" gag. "Shelly, come pull my finger!" he'd call out, and every time I did, he'd fart, sending us both into fits of laughter. Despite his playful side, his word was law. I never talked back to my dad, not even up to the day he died at the age of 92 two years ago.

My dad was an introvert, a trait he passed on to me. Despite his quiet nature, he was an enthusiastic grandfather. He even quit drinking, something he had done the majority of his life, to take care of my boys so they wouldn't have to go to daycare. He knew he would have zero chance of keeping them if he continued to drink. He attended every sporting event and church activity they were involved in despite his own lack of belief.

His dad was a Bishop in the Church of God in Christ and often used the scripture in Proverbs 13:24, which states, "Whoever spares the rod hates his son, but he who loves him is diligent to discipline him," to abuse my dad and his four brothers. He would beat them for hours at a time for small infractions, such as playing in the street. My dad grew up loathing Christianity and everything it stood for.

That was not the intent of that scripture, and it turned my dad against God for the rest of his life, or so he led us to believe. He often bragged to others about his kids being saved, so only God knows.

When my parents divorced, I felt like my dad divorced me too because of a secret we weren't told, like my mother's restraining order against him, which only deepened the rift. Heartbroken, he moved away from Colorado.

One vivid memory from my teens surrounding my dad was the day I was working at The Grove, a nut shop at the airport. One day, I saw my dad walking down the concourse. "Hey, Dad! Where are you going?" I called out. He replied, "Didn't your mom tell you? I'm moving to California." He shook my hand and said, "Have a good life." I was devastated. I cried for three seconds before turning off my emotions, much to the shock of my coworkers. They rushed to me with a caring embrace and asked was I ok. I wiped my tears, told them I was fine, and returned to my duties as if nothing happened.

When I was burned by my car radiator, a story revealed in this book, my dad moved back to Colorado to care for me. He rented a duplex, which was a 5 minute drive from my mother's house, and bought me a new car. I admit it, I am very spoiled because of my dad, and my husband picked up that mantle and ran with it.

I was with him the day he died. He knew it was his time and told me that the hospital visit would be his last. On October 22, 2022, he passed away. I looked death straight in the eye for the first time in my life and saw he wasn't there. I was intrigued and saddened at the same time. God showed me it wasn't him while missing him in tandem.

I have Pulmonary Arterial Hypertension (PAH). A Nurse Practitioner advised me not to grieve too hard, warning it could endanger my own health. While I understood her intent, it wasn't right for me. This advice led me to compartmentalize my grief. I put my feelings into a box, only opening it when I passed by his apartment or saw a picture of him. The pain was intense and debilitating each time, like his death happened that very day, that moment. Eventually, I realized this wasn't healthy. I had to grieve my dad's death. I had to unwrap the box and feel every pain of his passing. This approach may not work for all PAH patients, but it was what I needed.

My mom, an extrovert, had a difficult upbringing. Raised by her father after her mother left her at the tender young age of four, faced stern discipline from her father, neglect from some of her extended family, and physical abuse from her first husband. Despite these challenges, she was a dedicated provider, working three jobs to support us after her divorce from my father. While she was verbally abusive and often critical, her maternal instincts shone through when I was sick. She pampered me and treated me with so much love that I yearned for on a daily basis but did not receive it. I'm not saying she didn't love me. However, the daily abusive language overshadowed everything else.

The message I learned from this experience was that people show you love when you're sick; until they get tired of you, that is. I learned the latter part years later. In turn I grew up thinking being sick was a good thing. Even to this day, while I constantly fight the battle of a terminal illness, I suppress the feelings of comfort in being ill. The child within in me still yearns for the attention, while the adult knows there is something far greater at hand. What a complex web of turmoil.

Through Christ and counseling, I'm gaining victory. Why is it taking so long? It took 55 years for me to admit my truth. My husband was the first person I told a month ago. Can't fix what you don't admit!

My mom taught me the importance of presenting oneself well, though as a tomboy, I didn't appreciate it until much later. She taught me how to be a lady at all times and how to cater to my husband. Lessons I'm sure she learned from her father.

I have some wonderful memories with my mom that are seared in my mind as an adult. Like lying in bed with her, talking and laughing for hours. Planning my wedding and her knowing the perfect dress for me, paying no attention to the cost. Her prayers over me kept me safe when she felt in her spirit that something was wrong, whether mentally or physically, with me. We are attached that way. Her prayers are powerful!

As I got older, I started speaking up for myself so that's when the fights started. She didn't back down, and neither did I. Her verbal abuse stopped towards me in March of 2023, when we were ripped from each other's arms due to her illness. She had to be moved to another state, and our hearts broke. She has not said one unkind word towards me since. My heart is so full of love for her that I can't contain it. She tells me how proud she is of me, how beautiful I am, and to never forget what she has taught me. She is about to turn 96 now, and our relationship is beautiful. No regrets and no unforgiveness in my heart.

Through it all, she is my best friend. I could talk to her about anything. I can't anymore; she is ill and has dementia.

No more lying in bed next to her, laughing and talking for hours. That's what I miss the most. I would lay my head on her shoulder like I was five years old again.

The sexual abuse I endured from a family friend starting at the age of five further compounded my struggles. Our parents allowed us to take baths together at a young age. She would molest me while we were bathing. The abuse then would transfer to the bedroom, where she would wake me up out of my slumber to molest me.

Even at the age of five, I found it pleasurable. So I never told anyone while it was happening at her behest and the pleasure I felt. I didn't reveal this to my parents until I was 45, and even then, my parents didn't believe me. Looking back, I'm grateful I didn't tell them earlier; the pain would have been unbearable.

What she did to me caused a lot of problems for me sexually. I was confused and felt like I had done something wrong. The disgust I felt took a toll on me as I got older. The disgust turned into victimization as being touched in a sexual manner as an adult made my skin crawl at times. I found solace in drinking a glass of wine to ease the anxiety.

As time went on and the child within me began to scream to be heard, making love to my husband felt like rape if I didn't initiate it. He understood and accepted me as I was, no questions asked.

My husband, whom I've been married to for 33 years, is a wonderful, loving, and caring man—truly an answer to my prayers. He's a retired First Sergeant from the Air Force for 27 years and a retired Policeman for 31 years. We certainly have our issues, but our communication skills are profound. Having God at the center of our lives and our home certainly makes the difference.

Early on, I tried to push him away, fearing he would eventually leave like everyone else, but he assured me he never would, and he hasn't. His unwavering love and support, especially through my trials and tribulations, have been a testament to his strength and dedication to me and, more importantly, God.

After being diagnosed with Chronic Regional Pain Syndrome (CRPS), my depression worsened, leading to five suicide attempts. Each time, I managed to convince others it was just a bad day. The constant, inexplicable depression and the constant, unrelenting pain I felt were a daily battle. Until one day, at the age of 60, in the shower—my place of refuge—I cried out to the Lord. Tears streaming down my face, I prayed for His presence, begging for a personal relationship with Him, "Oh God, just like Jacob! I won't let go until you bless me!"

That's when I heard His voice. He promised never to leave me or forsake me, assuring me of His love for me. From that moment, I was transformed. My relationship with God became real and personal. Not just the Deity I had read and studied about in my latter years in Bible study and in my own personal study time. I had experienced Him for myself. It makes all the difference in your Christian walk. I haven't experienced depression since that day, and a year later, I am renewed. Old things have passed away, and all things have become new.

Chapter Two

"Is anyone among you suffering? Let him pray. Is anyone cheerful? Let him sing praise. Is anyone among you sick? Let him call for the elders of the church, and let them pray over him, anointing him with oil in the name of the Lord." (James 5:13-14)

In the summer of 1981, I stood at the threshold of adulthood, eager to carve out my own path in the world. Fresh out of high school, with college on the horizon, I felt a heady mix of excitement and apprehension coursing through my veins.

It was during those final days of freedom before the academic grind would take hold that fate intervened, leading me down a path I never could have imagined. My mother, ever the practical one, secured me a job at the Denver Public Schools Film Library, where she herself worked—a small act of maternal guidance that would have far-reaching consequences.

It was there, amidst the shelves of dusty reels and flickering projectors, that I first laid eyes on Mark—a tall, handsome figure with a smile that could light up a room. Our meeting was unremarkable at first, just two strangers passing in the fluorescent-lit halls of bureaucracy. But as the days wore on, a connection blossomed—a spark of curiosity and attraction that refused to be ignored.

It was on a sweltering August evening, after a week of casual banter and stolen glances that Mark asked me for a ride home.

My mother's words echoed in my mind as I drove Mark home against her wishes. She had sternly reminded me that she footed the bill for my car's gas and adamantly asserted that Mark was simply too lazy to change his own tire. But at seventeen, rebellion tasted sweeter than reason, and I brushed aside her concerns with a stubborn resolve.

As we pulled up to his house, Mark extended an invitation inside, but I declined, citing the need to get home. After all, I wasn't about to compromise my principles for the sake of a fleeting moment. With a nod of understanding, he exited the car, leaving me to wrestle with the mechanical woes of my overheating engine. Just as expected, as I drove down the highway, my radiator began to overheat at 270°. Although I felt the frustration of this ongoing problem, I thought, "What a perfect plan. When I get home, I can change the water pump. Mom will think I was out front the whole time!" Needless to say, my mother saw me when I drove up.

As I began to remove the clamp on the water pump, I remembered I needed a special tool. I headed towards the backseat of the car to retrieve the tool, expecting to find it in the backseat where I knew I had left it. But, to my surprise, the tool wasn't there. Frustrated and knowing my mom would fuss at me, I started going up the stairs to the house.

However, something made me pause. Instead of facing my mom's inevitable lecture, I decided to check the car again. I went back to the backseat, and miraculously, the tool was right there on the seat where I had originally placed it.

In retrospect, I felt a profound realization wash over me. It was as if God had hidden the tool from me initially, but I was insistent upon being deceitful and decided to look again. He allowed me to find it. This moment was more than just about a tool.

With a tug on the water pump clip, disaster struck in a burst of scalding steam and antifreeze-laced boiling water. I gasped, and there was a two-second pause, and suddenly, pain seared through me like a white-hot poker, and I found myself running blindly, arms raised in a futile attempt to shield myself from the relentless onslaught.

A neighbor rushed to my aid, armed with a water hose and a heart full of concern. But fear held him back, hesitating to offer aid for fear of being misconstrued. It was only the arrival of a minister from across the street that brought a measure of relief—a gentle touch and a prayer offering solace in my hour of need.

With trembling hands and a heart heavy with shock, I stumbled into the safety of my home, where friends gathered to offer what little comfort they could.

As shock began to grip me, I pleaded to sit down, but my friends were trying to remove my clothes, causing more pain. Even my mom tried to help, but her efforts only made things worse. Shockingly, no one thought to call an ambulance. Instead, my mom's friend drove me to the hospital.

As I sat in the car, the pain seemed to intensify with every passing second. The sun beat down mercilessly, exacerbating the already searing agony coursing through my body. While the antifreeze trapped the heat inside my blustering skin. Each stoplight felt like an eternity, every halt a cruel reminder of the precious minutes slipping away.

I pleaded with the driver to go faster, to run the lights if he had to, but my words fell on deaf ears. His reluctance to take risks only added to my frustration, amplifying the sense of helplessness that threatened to engulf me. With each passing mile, the blisters on my skin multiplied, increasing my pain and suffering. I could feel the heat radiating from my body, a relentless reminder of the ordeal I was enduring.

Finally, mercifully, we arrived at the hospital. But even as I stumbled towards the emergency room, I knew that the worst was far from over. The nurses rushed to my aid, their faces etched with concern as they assessed the extent of my injuries. The nurses set to work, pouring cool water over my blistered skin in a desperate bid to ease my suffering. And for a fleeting moment, it worked—the cool liquid providing a brief respite from the torment.

But as the water ceased to flow, the pain returned with a vengeance. Despite their best efforts, the nurses struggled to alleviate my suffering, their expressions mirroring my own sense of desperation.

The pain was unbearable. No matter how much morphine the doctors gave me, nothing seemed to help. They tried everything, but I still hurt so much. It felt like the pain would never end.

Then my mother came into the room. She was calm and determined. Without saying a word, she took out a small bottle of oil. She gently anointed my forehead and began to pray. Her voice was steady and soothing, each word filled with love and faith. She prayed for my healing, for peace, and for the pain to go away.

As she prayed, I felt a strange and wonderful calmness wash over me. The pain that had been so fierce began to fade. I felt peaceful for the first time in what felt like forever. My eyes grew heavy, and I knew I was about to fall asleep.

Before I drifted off, I accepted the Lord into my life. In that quiet moment, my mother's prayers had done what the doctors' medicine couldn't. They brought me comfort and peace. Her faith had become my own, and I finally felt at ease.

When I woke up, I was being moved to a different hospital. I peeked under the blanket and saw my burns—they looked horrific. Hundreds of tiny blisters covered my body, with a huge one that extended the length of my right forearm. But the doctor said not to worry, that I'd be out of the hospital in a week. It turned out to be a month.

I was confused by what I saw, though. It wasn't just how I looked; it was something I'd seen in my dreams for months. God was trying to tell me something, and I finally understood. The blisters covering me were just like what I'd seen before in my dreams.

At the new hospital, they put me in a special tent to protect me from infection. Then they said I could go to physical therapy in a Jacuzzi. I was excited. I even joked with my friends how I was going to chill in the jacuzzi tomorrow, but it wasn't what I expected. They put me in the Jacuzzi and started popping all my blisters. It hurt so much, and I had to lie in the pus-filled water.

They did this twice a day, using tweezers to pull off my damaged skin. It was painful, but I tried to laugh with my friends afterward about it. Because I was in so much pain, a Doctor asked me if I was receiving pain meds before the debriding—removing the damaged skin—process. I told him no. He made sure I had them from that day forward. I was quite taken aback, knowing that I didn't have to suffer the intensity of pain I was feeling. I was literally being tortured, to say the least.

After a month of this, my hands looked white, and the doctor said they might stay that way. But I knew they wouldn't. Over time, they turned brown again. The hospital used a cream called Silvadene on my burns. It served as a temporary skin until mine healed. It stopped the pain. However, when they applied the Silvadene cream, it ended up causing more harm. They spread it too thickly, so when it came time for debriding, it made the process even more painful. The tongue depressor they used to scrape it off felt like torture against my raw flesh.

But in the middle of the agony, I learned an important lesson: when my skin bled during the debriding process, it was a sign of healing. It was a stark reminder that things that bleed aren't dead—a truth I learned the hard way.

Stuck in the hospital for a month, I felt like I was losing my mind. I longed to escape the confines of my room, to feel the sun on my skin and the touch of another human being. But the pain kept me trapped, isolated from the world outside.

I reached out to my mom for comfort, but even she couldn't bear to see me in so much pain, not to mention the smell of burnt flesh in my room. It was a lonely, despairing time, and I found myself sinking into depression. I felt like I had lost a part of myself, like I was no longer whole. My mom's reassurances offered little solace, but I clung to them nonetheless.

As I was finally released from the hospital, I thought the worst was behind me. Little did I know, the road to recovery was just beginning? The nerve regeneration process brought a whole new level of pain, driving me to scratch at my skin until it bled.

The Doctors ordered a Jobst vest designed to add pressure to burn scars or keloids to flatten the surface area. I was supposed to wear it 24/7 for the keloids that had developed severely on my abdomen and breast. The vest was too painful for me to tolerate, so I chose not to wear it. Thus, the keloids became a massive sheet across the burn area.

Physically, it took a year for me to heal, but mentally, the scars ran much deeper. I struggled with PTSD, reliving the events of that fateful day over and over again in my mind. But with no help and no support, I had to find a way to cope on my own.

Looking back, I realized the price I paid for my disobedience. The scars I bore would serve as a constant reminder of the consequences of my actions. It was a heavy burden to bear, one that I would carry for the rest of my life.

But through the pain and the suffering, I found solace in my newfound faith. It was in those darkest moments that my faith in God began to take root—a beacon of hope in a world filled with pain and uncertainty.

I started college that fall, still healing and in a tremendous amount of pain. This was my introduction to opioids. I slowly put my faith on the back burner due to the stress of being in college under those circumstances. My grades were dropping, and I received my first "F." I was devastated! My life took a turn for the better when I met a young lady by the name of Cyn, who, unbeknownst to me, would become and still is a paramount figure in my life. We very quickly became close friends, the best of friends. One day, I stayed the night at her house because we were going out to Scooters (a youth night club) that Saturday night. Cyn had one rule she stood by religiously, and she made me stand by it, too. "Shell!" She said with a stern voice. I quickly took note of her change of demeanor. "If we go out tonight, no matter how late we get in, we have to go to church in the morning!" I agreed; the serious look on her face didn't leave me with much of a choice.

Cyn didn't know I had slipped back into my old habits after I had healed from my burns. God used her as a catalyst to draw me back into His arms. In the church she took me to, I joined and got baptized. Most importantly, I experienced the power of the Holy Spirit.

Church became my life. I joined two other churches after joining Cyn's church. Each church caters to different stages of my walk. All of them were profound in my life, adding growth and a deeper understanding of Christ. The first church is where I experienced the Holy Spirit and sang on our first album. In the second church, I received foundational teaching and my first experience of having a church family and a Pastor who ushered me into my destiny by noticing my gifts. His pastorship not only increased my spiritual growth but also gave me the opportunity to get promoted to administrative secretary because he made me his secretary at church. The third church taught me the importance of serving others through outreach, singing on a praise team, and doing plays, and I sang on another album. All of which were totally out of my character. They all helped me develop who I am today, and I will always love and cherish them in my heart.

Chapter Three

It was a typical Saturday night, and my neighbors and I had plans to go to a house party. We were 17, full of youthful bravado, and eager for a bit of adventure. The party was about 12 blocks away, and we set out around 9:00 PM walking. I knew I shouldn't be going—I was too young, and my gut told me to stay home. But the thrill of rebellion and the promise of a fun night out outweighed my better judgment.

As we arrived at the house, the music was already pumping, and the basement was filled with the hazy smoke of marijuana. The air was thick, and I could feel the fumes making their way into my lungs. I coughed and choked on the smoke, feeling the effects of the marijuana seep into my system. My friends and I talked and danced to a couple of songs, trying to ignore the growing discomfort.

Just then, an older gentleman asked me to dance. It was a slow dance, and as the marijuana began to affect me more, I found myself clumsily stepping on his feet. He pulled me closer, saying, "It's just me, baby." When I looked up, I realized he was much older than I was—probably ten years older, with a toothless grin that made my stomach churn. I knew I shouldn't be dancing with him. Feeling a wave of nausea and discomfort, I told my friends I was ready to leave.

But they weren't ready to go. Frustrated and determined, I made a reckless decision to walk home by myself. It was about 1:00 in the morning, and darkness had settled over everything. The cold night air bit at my skin and a deep sense of unease settled in my chest. I couldn't turn back; the party had disgusted me, and I was convinced I could make it home.

The streets were eerily quiet, with only the occasional sound of distant cars or rustling leaves breaking the silence. Each step echoed in the stillness, amplifying my fear. My heart raced, and I quickened my pace, desperate to reach the safety of my home.

When I was just three blocks away from my house, a car with four men pulled up beside me. I kept my head down and walked briskly, hoping they would leave me alone. They rolled down the windows, and one of them called out, "Hey baby, come get in the car with us."

Panic surged through me. "No, thank you," I mumbled, not breaking my stride.

"Don't be like that," another man said. "Don't make us have to come and get you."

My heart pounded harder, each beat resonating in my ears. Suddenly, I heard a car door open. Before I could fully process what was happening, my instincts kicked in. I sprinted faster than I ever had before towards my house. It felt like I was running at warp speed, my legs pumping with adrenaline. I didn't look back, and within moments, I was on my front porch, gasping for breath. The men had barely gotten back in their car before I was out of their reach, and they sped off without pursuing me further.

Trembling, I opened the door. My mother was standing there, her face a mix of relief and concern. "I just finished praying for you," she said softly.

I collapsed into her arms, tears streaming down my face. "I never want to go to another house party in my life," I vowed, clinging to her for dear life.

That night, I learned a harsh lesson about trust, safety, and the importance of listening to my instincts. It was an experience that stayed with me forever, shaping the choices I made and the paths I followed. Never again did I let the thrill of rebellion overshadow the voice of reason within me.

Chapter Four

"The Lord himself watches over you! The Lord stands beside you as your protective shade." (Psalm 121:5)

It was a snowy day in Colorado, and my roommate, Lisa, and I decided to drive from the University of Colorado in Boulder to Denver to visit our boyfriends. The weather forecast had predicted light snow, but it seemed manageable. We thought nothing could go wrong with a short trip for a night of fun in the city. After all, we had driven in light snow many times before.

The night in Denver was everything we hoped it would be—warm laughter, shared stories, and the joy of being with our boyfriends. By the next morning, we reluctantly packed our bags to head back to campus, only to be greeted by a harsh reality: the light snow had transformed into a full-blown snowstorm overnight.

Lisa and I exchanged anxious looks as we loaded the car. The thick flakes fell steadily, and the wind howled, shaking the trees and reducing visibility to almost nothing. Driving back to Boulder was going to be more challenging than we had anticipated, but we had to get back to class. With a sense of determination, we bundled up, cranked up the car, and set off.

As we merged onto I-70, the intensity of the storm increased. The road was covered in a blanket of snow, and our visibility was reduced to a few feet in front of the car. We drove cautiously, our breaths fogging up the windows despite the heater running at full blast. Lisa's hands gripped the steering wheel tightly, and every muscle in her body tensed with anxiety.

"Do you think we'll make it back?" I asked, my voice filled with worry.

"We have to," Lisa replied, trying to sound more confident than she felt. "We'll just take it slow."

Suddenly, we noticed a car ahead of us, its taillights barely visible through the snow. It was a sleek, black sedan, and it was moving erratically. At first, I thought the driver might be struggling with the road conditions, but it soon became clear that he was driving recklessly on purpose.

"What's he doing?" Lisa exclaimed, leaning forward to get a better look.

The driver was sliding from side to side, his tires skidding across the icy road as if his car had ice skating blades. It was as if he was on an ice rink, and he seemed to be enjoying himself, completely oblivious to the danger he was causing.

"Idiot," Lisa muttered under her breath. "He's going to get someone killed."

Our anger at the reckless driver grew with each passing minute. It was infuriating to watch someone treat these dangerous conditions like a game. The snowstorm was bad enough without having to worry about some fool who thought he was invincible.

But then, our anger turned to fear. The black sedan swerved dangerously close to our lane, and I could feel our car being pulled into his chaotic path. My heart pounded in my chest, and a cold sweat formed on Lisa's palms.

"Lisa, slow down," I whispered, my voice trembling.

"I'm trying," she replied, her throat tight with anxiety. She eased off the gas, hoping to put some distance between us and the maniac in front of us. But the roads were too slick, and every time she tried to slow down, the car seemed to slide more.

Suddenly, the black sedan slammed on its brakes, and everything seemed to happen in slow motion. The car spun out of control, its tires throwing up a spray of snow as it went into a tailspin. For a moment, I thought it was going to crash into us.

"Hold on!" Lisa shouted, gripping the wheel with all her strength.

Lisa screamed as our car slid to the right. The world tilted, and the snow enveloped us in a blinding flurry. We hit the embankment, and from our viewpoint, it looked like we were going over the edge, which had an intersecting street underneath. Panic surged through me, and I was certain that our decision to leave college to sneak down to Denver had been a mistake—one that could cost us our lives.

"God, no!" I thought, my mind racing with fear. "This can't be the end."

Suddenly, there was a loud smash, and the car jerked to a stop. We had hit the guardrail. I let out a shaky breath, my heart still pounding in my ears. The guardrail had saved us from going over the edge. We had come through the ordeal with minor injuries. Lisa had hurt her leg, and I had a minor case of whiplash, but we were alive.

As I rubbed my neck, trying to process what had just happened, I looked to my right and was astonished at what I saw. A massive diesel truck was right at my door, so close that I couldn't open it even an inch. Miraculously, it hadn't touched us. It was as if an invisible barrier had stopped it from hitting us.

"Lisa, look at this," I said, my voice shaking with disbelief.

Lisa turned and gasped. "Oh my God. How is that possible?"

I had to crawl out of the driver's side door to exit the vehicle. As we stood outside, gazing at the accident scene, we were even more amazed at the multiple cars that had run into the back of the diesel. It was a multiple-car pileup, and we had walked away from it.

"My God!" I whispered, tears streaming down my face. "Thy hand has once again saved me. For what? There has to be a greater purpose."

As we stood there, shaking from the cold and the shock, I couldn't help but feel that there was a reason we had been spared. The snowstorm raged on around us, but inside, I felt a strange sense of peace. We had survived, and I was determined to find out why.

This experience had changed me. It had shown me the fragility of life and the power of faith. As we waited for help to arrive, I silently promised myself that I would live my life with purpose and gratitude, knowing that there was a reason we had been given a second chance.

Chapter Five

I remember the day vividly. After undergoing surgery on my right wrist to have a ganglion cyst removed, I was discharged and sent home the same day. However, by the time I got home, the pain was unbearable, and my hand had swollen to twice its normal size. I called the on-call physician, hoping for some guidance or relief. His response was dismissive: "Chill out and go to sleep."

The next day, I went to the physical therapy room as instructed. The therapist took one look at my swollen hand and decided that physical therapy was out of the question. She referred me to a neurologist, who diagnosed me with Reflex Sympathetic Dystrophy (RSD). Today, this condition is known as Chronic Regional Pain Syndrome (CRPS), a rare, chronic, and incurable pain condition believed to be caused by the overreaction of the Sympathetic Nervous System following an injury or trauma to a limb.

The neurologist was adamant about the seriousness of CRPS and the need for aggressive treatment. I was immediately placed on a regimen of blood pressure pills and steroids for a week. The swelling subsided, leading the neurologist to believe that I might not have CRPS after all. However, two weeks later, the pain and swelling returned with a vengeance.

I was referred to another neurologist, who, unsure of the diagnosis, began administering cortisone injections into my wrist. The results were temporary at best. After several unsuccessful attempts, the doctor decided to perform more nerve blocks, again with limited success. The key to managing CRPS is early detection and treatment, but the uncertainty among the doctors delayed my definitive diagnosis for over a year. Dismissing all hope of a cure for this disease.

Frustrated and in constant pain, I insisted on seeing a new neurologist. Finally, this new doctor confirmed the CRPS diagnosis and scheduled me for a stellate ganglion block. This procedure involved administering conscious sedation and injecting lidocaine into my neck to calm the nerves. Unfortunately, the doctor performed the procedure blindly without using a fluoroscope to ensure the needle was in the correct spot.

After two years of enduring this treatment, the doctor missed the nerve and injected the lidocaine directly into my lungs. I couldn't breathe and was unable to communicate my distress. I thought I was dying. The nurse monitoring my oxygen levels noticed a drastic drop in my oxygen levels and began breathing for me using an Ambu bag while another medication was administered to counteract the lidocaine.

Despite the traumatic experience, I had to return the next day for the same procedure, this time performed under fluoroscopy to ensure accuracy. After three or four more of these injections, my neurologist decided to stop performing them and referred me to a pain specialist. The pain doctor evaluated my condition and determined that I was a candidate for a Spinal Cord Stimulator (SCS).

The SCS was to be placed at the level of my C6-C7 vertebrae, with wires running down to my hip and attached to a battery pack. This device would send signals to my brain to block the pain signals, functioning like an internal TENS unit. I was given a controller to adjust the intensity and preset programs for different coverage areas.

On the day of the surgery, I was filled with both hope and fear. The idea of a device that could potentially alleviate my pain was enticing, but the thought of another invasive procedure was daunting. My husband held my hand as I was wheeled into the operating room, whispering prayers and words of encouragement. The surgical team assured me that everything would go smoothly, and before I knew it, the anesthesia took effect, and I drifted into unconsciousness.

Waking up from the surgery, I felt a mixture of discomfort and relief. The incision sites were tender, but I could already tell that the SCS was having some effect. Over the next few days, I learned how to use the controller to adjust the settings, experimenting with different programs to find the most effective one for my pain.

For a while, it seemed like the SCS was the miracle solution I had been hoping for. My pain levels were more manageable, and I started to regain some semblance of a normal life. However, as with many things in life, initial success was not without complications.

A year after the surgery, I started experiencing issues with the battery pack. It was causing some discomfort and occasional sharp pains, making it difficult to sit or lie down for extended periods. The pain specialist informed me that this was a known issue and recommended another surgery to relocate the battery pack to a more comfortable position.

The second surgery went smoothly, and the battery pack was successfully moved to my lower back. This time, the recovery process was quicker, and I experienced less discomfort from the new location. However, as the years went by, the SCS required further attention. Technological advancements led to upgrades in the device, and I had to undergo additional surgeries for repairs and updates.

Throughout this journey, my relationship with my medical team evolved. I became more knowledgeable about my condition and the treatments available, and I learned to advocate for myself more effectively. I also found strength in my faith and the support of my loved ones, especially my husband, who was my rock during the most challenging times.

Living with CRPS has taught me many lessons about resilience, perseverance, and the importance of self-advocacy. It's a daily battle, but one that I face with determination and hope. Each surgery, each setback, and each moment of relief has been a part of this complex journey. I continue to seek new treatments and stay informed about the latest advancements in pain management, always striving for a better quality of life despite the chronic pain that accompanies me.

In the quiet moments, when the pain becomes overwhelming, I find solace in prayer and reflection. I remind myself of the times when I thought I couldn't go on, only to find the strength to persevere. My faith has been a guiding light, providing comfort and hope when the medical treatments fall short.

As I look back on the years of struggle and triumph, I am reminded of the importance of listening to my body and trusting my instincts. The journey with CRPS is far from over, but I am determined to face each new challenge with courage and faith. Through the ups and downs, I hold on to the belief that there is always hope for a better tomorrow.

Chapter Six

I was in a relationship for approximately seven years. We were engaged to be married, but we decided to put it on hold because things weren't going well at that time. I agreed we would see other people to keep him in my life. This went against everything I believed in, but I loved him so much that I was willing to do anything to keep him around.

One Friday, we went to happy hour at a bar called Pierre's with a group of friends. We were all sitting at a long table when a young lady whom I had prior problems with. She asked him when he was coming to visit her in Colorado Springs. He casually replied, "As soon as I get paid." Shocked, I tapped him and asked what he was talking about. He reminded me of our agreement. I felt a wave of embarrassment but shook it off, not realizing the extent of his interpretation of our agreement.

Things escalated quickly when he asked her to dance. It was a fast song, so I decided to dance with a young man who asked me. However, when a slow song began, I stopped dancing out of respect for my boyfriend. But seeing him take her into his arms for a slow dance made me furious. That was the last straw.

I approached him and asked angrily if we could talk outside. He seemed annoyed and said, "Michelle, see, this is what I'm talking about." As soon as we reached outside, my anger exploded. I began hitting him out of a deep well of pent-up emotions fueled by the alcohol that was in my system. He tried to stop me, never hitting back, just trying to restrain me.

All the pain and anger I had bottled up over the years came out in those moments. I hit him for every time I felt inadequate, for the abuse I had endured in my past, for every man who made me feel ugly, for every moment I felt less than enough. My fury, coupled with my drunken state, pushed us to the ground, setting off a car alarm.

The police arrived quickly. An officer grabbed me, pinning my arms behind my back, which was excruciating because of my CRPS. I kept telling her she was hurting me, but she dismissed my pain, assuming I was just another drunk causing trouble. As she walked me to the police car, I pleaded with her, "Please don't take me to jail. I'm involved in a security clearance right now, and you will ruin my life!" Miraculously, she stopped, as if there was a wall there, just short of her police car door, and released me to my boyfriend and told him to take me straight home. She released me to the man I was just fiercely fighting with? It was nothing short of the grace and mercy of God in action.

The next day, I was feeling extremely low. I knew I had blown whatever chance I had left with my boyfriend. Hoping to clear my mind, I dressed and went to a nearby park. There, I met two guys who started talking about the crazy drunk girl from the night before who beat up her boyfriend. Awkwardly, I confessed that it was me, and we laughed about it. This unexpected encounter led to me dating one of the guys months later.

Despite this new relationship, I quickly found myself in a precarious situation. The two men I had befriended were drug dealers. One day, someone knocked on the door asking if we were "holding," a term I didn't understand. Oblivious, I said no and closed the door. It wasn't until later that I realized what I had what I had walked into when one of them started freebasing in the living room. When offered some, I declined, and my new boyfriend's roommate defended me, saying, "No, she's not that type of girl. She doesn't need this stuff."

I was a person who loved easily and without judgment, but I knew I had to get out of this situation quickly. One night, my new boyfriend claimed he was too sick to go to Scooters, a nightclub in Colorado. I went anyway and saw him there, healthy and dancing. That was the final straw. I walked away from him, and that dangerous situation was just as easy as I had entered it.

Looking back, I realize the immense power of grace and mercy in my life. From the police officer's unexpected compassion to the realization of the dangerous path I was on, I see how I was guided and protected. These experiences have given me a deeper understanding of my own worth and the courage to stand up for myself, even when it's difficult.

Today, I am more mindful of the relationships I nurture and the choices I make. I have learned to prioritize my well-being and to recognize when it's time to walk away. The scars from those days serve as reminders of my resilience and the journey I have undertaken to become the person I am now. Through it all, my faith and the support of my loved ones have been my anchor, helping me navigate the complexities of life with grace and strength.

Chapter Seven

It was an ordinary day, the kind where nothing seemed out of the ordinary until everything changed in a heartbeat. I was walking down the stairs, thinking about what I needed to do next. The house was quiet, the kind of calm that makes you feel like all is right with the world. The sun filtered through the curtains, casting a warm glow on the wooden floors. I had just taken a step when I missed the bottom stairs. In an instant, I felt myself falling, my arms flailing to grab onto something, anything. But there was nothing to hold onto, and I landed hard, spraining both of my ankles.

Pain shot through my legs like a lightning bolt, and I couldn't hold back the scream that escaped my lips. I remember lying there, clutching my ankles, tears streaming down my face. The pain was intense, a sharp, throbbing agony that made it hard to think. I called out for my husband, my voice shaky and desperate. He came running, his face a mask of concern and fear. He helped me to the car, and we drove to the doctor's office, each bump in the road sending waves of pain through my body.

At the doctor's office, they examined my ankles and decided to put splints on both of them. The splints were tight and uncomfortable, but they provided some much-needed stability. The doctor told me I needed to wear them for a while to let my ankles heal. I nodded, trying to focus on his words through the haze of pain.

Days turned into weeks, and the weeks into months, and the splints were eventually replaced by braces. The braces were bulky and awkward, making it hard to move around. I felt like a prisoner in my own body, each step a reminder of my limitations. I tried to stay positive, but it was hard. The pain was a constant companion, always there, lurking in the background.

I have Chronic Regional Pain Syndrome (CRPS), a condition that amplifies pain signals in the body. It's like having a volume knob on pain that is turned all the way up. I was already seeing a pain management doctor for that, and he noticed I was still in the braces after a long time. He offered to do further studies to see if there was something else going on.

The days were long and difficult. The weather outside was beautiful, the sun shining and the birds singing, but it felt like a cruel joke. I couldn't enjoy any of it. I spent most of my time inside, staring out the window, longing to be able to go for a walk or even just stand without pain. My husband was my rock, always there to help me, but I could see the strain it was putting on him, too.

One day, I started to experience a new kind of pain. It was a burning sensation on the lateral aspect of my knee, a sharp, searing pain that made it hard to even sit comfortably. My pain doctor recommended that I have a CT scan of my hip to see if there was something else causing the pain.

The CT scan showed that I had a cyst in my nerve canal and arthritis in my sacroiliac joint. It was another blow, another thing to add to the list of problems. The doctors decided to install a spinal cord stimulator, my second one, to help manage the pain. The stimulator would be placed on my lumbar spine, and the battery pack would be placed on my right hip.

On the day of the surgery, I was hopeful. I thought maybe this would be the thing that finally helped, that gave me some relief. The surgery went well, and I was sent home to recover. But the next day, I was in severe pain. It was a pain like nothing I had ever experienced before. It felt like hot pokers were being jammed into my neck, an excruciating, unrelenting agony that left me screaming and crying.

The pain was worse when I tried to get out of bed or even hold my head up. Each step was more excruciating than the last. My husband had to help me to the bathroom. I would grab both his hands and shuffle, screaming and crying, begging him to go faster so I could get it over with. All I wanted was to get back to bed, where the pain would stop.

It took us a while to get a hold of the doctor. When we finally did, my husband explained how much pain I was in. The doctor called in a prescription, but it did absolutely nothing. Any other attempts to contact him were futile. We could only assume he thought I was drug-seeking because he ignored us from that point on. The pain continued for two more days, and just when I thought I couldn't take it any longer, it suddenly ceased. The relief was overwhelming as if a weight had been lifted off my chest. I lay in bed, exhausted and relieved, thankful that the worst was over.

On the seventh day after my surgery, I woke up with a sense of foreboding. I felt unusually tired and weak, as though something was not right. Brushing off the feeling, I decided to go downstairs, thinking a change of scenery might help. My son was in the den, absorbed in his video game, the colorful lights reflecting off his face.

As I passed by, he glanced up and asked, "Mom, are you okay?" His voice was tinged with concern.

I tried to respond, but the words came out garbled, like I was speaking a foreign language. Confused, he looked at me, but I could only manage to shake my head slightly before everything started spinning. A wave of dizziness hit me, my legs turned to jelly, and I collapsed to the ground, a feeling of malaise washing over my body.

Panic surged through me. I knew I had to do something, but my body wasn't responding. My son's voice sounded distant as he called my husband, who was at church. "Dad, you need to come home! Something's wrong with Mom!"

He ran upstairs and found me unconscious in front of his bedroom door. He mustered all his strength to pick me up and carry me to my bed. My husband arrived home in record time, his face etched with worry. He placed an oxygen mask on my nose, hoping it would stabilize me.

Even in my dazed state, I knew something was horribly wrong. But amidst the fear, there was a strange sense of peace and calmness. It was as if a comforting presence enveloped me. I mouthed to my husband and son, "Call 911. I'm dying."

The paramedics arrived quickly, their expressions serious as they took my vitals. "Her blood pressure is 90/20," one of them said, his tone urgent. Normal blood pressure is around 120/80, so mine was dangerously low.

As they rushed me to the hospital, the world around me began to fade. I lost consciousness somewhere along the way, and the next thing I remember was waking up in the emergency room. The first thing I saw was a CT scan of my lungs on the wall. A doctor's voice pierced through my foggy mind, "She's waking up."

I was placed on a heparin drip to prevent further clotting and was transferred to the ICU. It felt surreal to sit up and talk to my family and friends as if nothing had happened. They were astonished, their faces a mix of relief and disbelief. The doctors explained to them about the massive saddle clot that had formed in my lungs. By all medical reasoning, I should not have survived. They had no explanations, only that it was a miracle I was alive.

I spent four days in the ICU, each day feeling like a gift. The nurses monitored me closely, and their care and compassion were constant sources of comfort. Eventually, I was moved to the main hospital, where I stayed for another three days. During this time, I was still under close watch. I wasn't able to use the bathroom on my own and had to rely on a portable potty. Showering was out of the question without assistance, which was incredibly uncomfortable but necessary.

Despite the discomfort and the indignity of having someone observe my every move, I felt profoundly grateful. This was yet another miracle where I felt God had intervened in my life. I remembered a passage from the Bible, "Death, take your hands off my child!" It felt like those words had come true for me.

One afternoon, a young medical student came into my room. His eyes were wide, and he had a mix of awe and curiosity. "I had to meet you," he said. "In medical school, they taught us that people with massive saddle clots usually don't survive. But here you are, a true miracle."

He explained how the clot had been blocking the openings of both my lungs, making it almost impossible for blood to flow through. "I don't know how you survived," he said, shaking his head.

I smiled at him and said, "I know how I survived. God kept me. He's the reason I'm still here."

Three times now, I had faced death and survived against all odds. Some people never experience one miracle in their lives, and here I was, living through my third. It was humbling and awe-inspiring.

Chapter Eight

After the ordeal with my wrist surgery and the subsequent struggles with CRPS, I thought I had faced the worst. But life had another challenge in store. A few years after I began managing CRPS, and during the diagnosis of the blood clot in my lungs, they discovered another severe condition—Pulmonary Arterial Hypertension (PAH).

It all started when my doctors noticed I had high pressure in my lungs. Normal pressures are below 20, but mine were at a staggering 75. Despite the urgency of the situation, it took them almost six or seven months to start treatment, giving me time to heal from the clot. At my first appointment, the doctor explained I had PAH, a terminal illness characterized by high blood pressure in the lungs that damages the arteries. This damage causes pressure to build up in the right side of the heart, leading to heart failure. He explained it was likely due to my sleep apnea, but there was another unknown cause, making it Idiopathic PAH. He also mentioned that although it was rare and there was no cure, significant strides in research meant people were living longer with the disease.

As the doctor explained PAH to me, I felt he was sugarcoating things and not telling me everything. When I started treatment, I was assigned a Nurse Practitioner. She was a high-spirited, fun-loving, and honest lady who soon became a good friend. I saw her more than my doctor, and she essentially became my healthcare provider. Her knowledge far exceeded that of a typical nurse practitioner, and I often told her she should have been a doctor.

One day, I asked her blatantly if I was dying. She told me yes but emphasized that PAH patients write their own stories, and she couldn't tell me when. I appreciated her honesty and asked her always to be straightforward with me. She agreed.

Initially, my symptoms weren't too bad. They told me I probably had PAH long before it was discovered. Seven years earlier, I had noticed when I sang in the choir, my breath would fade away abruptly. I mentioned it to my doctor, but he didn't take me seriously, even asked me to sing in front of him, which made me nervous. He ignored my complaint and did nothing. I kept insisting, and they finally put me on oxygen to appease me. Unknowingly, this oxygen therapy saved my life.

Over time, my condition worsened. I ended up on oxygen 24/7. My heart started racing at the slightest effort of movement. I couldn't go from my bed to my bathroom without my heart rate soaring to 130 beats per minute. My world shrank to my bedroom for over seven years. I could no longer attend church or hang out with friends. My life revolved around doctors' appointments, echocardiograms, and cardiac catheterizations. The cardiac catheters were terrifying, involving a needle in my neck, replaced with plastic tubing, and a camera inserted into my jugular vein to view my heart.

Being at a teaching hospital added to the anxiety. I often overheard doctors instructing students with phrases like, "Back up, you're in the wrong spot," while a tube was in my jugular vein. Anxiety medication didn't work on me due to my long history with pain meds, making these experiences even more harrowing. The skin on my neck developed keloids, giving me the appearance of being bitten by a vampire after each procedure, except when handled by more experienced doctors. I've had six of these procedures now, and they haven't gotten any easier for me.

In September of 2023, I started on a drug called Opsumit, which was being monitored by the FDA. I mentioned this in my PAH support group, and a form from the FDA popped up on my post, asking about my use and side effects. I felt violated but answered their questions. A week into taking Opsumit, I experienced severe fatigue and muscle aches in my legs. I contacted the pharmacy and my doctor, but he wasn't responding. Eventually, I told him about the side effects, and he advised me to hold on, saying they would go away. However, the side effects didn't go away; they worsened with flushing and blurry vision. After seven weeks, I couldn't take it anymore and left a message for my doctor, stating I was stopping the medication and needed advice on how to do it correctly. He never responded.

A couple of weeks later, I ended up in the hospital with fluid in my heart and lungs. I later found out that other Opsumit patients had similar experiences. I got into a heated argument with my doctor, expressing my anger at his lack of response. He defended his actions by saying he was busy with other patients and he wasn't my concierge. I was shocked and disheartened.

I spent five days in the hospital, reflecting on how this situation could have been avoided if my messages hadn't been ignored. Since then, I've moved to Virginia, where my PAH has advanced from mild to moderate, with lung pressure at 50. I've had to make significant changes in my life to accommodate this progression. I've come to accept that not all my friends will accompany me on this journey, but I'm grateful for those who do. I don't know what the future holds, but I trust in the one who holds my future.

My activity level has been greatly affected. I wear oxygen again, but not for my lungs; it's to support my heart, which is struggling to send blood through my body against the high pressures from my lungs. I have bouts of fatigue that rob me of my steps, like I have just run a 10-mile marathon, gasping for air that's not there. My weeks are filled with a minimum of three doctor visits a week, with some being twice on the same day. I carry 20 lbs of water weight consistently attached to every inch of my body, including my sinuses and ears. However, the massive fluid volume is in my stomach. My body is very sensitive to the drugs they give me, so I'm not being treated with the meds like most PAH patients are. A thought that leaves me contemplating my mortality and dealing with a lot of frustration.

I take 80mg of Viagra (Sildenafil) a day. Go ahead and laugh; I thought it was pretty funny, too. No, to answer your curious thoughts. Viagra opens up blood vessels, so it's a common drug for PAH patients.

I have lost many friends due to my illness. However, I have a strong inner circle now. People I can depend on, no matter what state of mind I'm in. There will come a time when I won't be able to function on my own. People see how great we look and sound and don't realize the severity and devastation of this disease. I fight daily to keep a smile on my face and to remain as normal as I possibly can be. When compared to the whirlwind that's going on inside, I'm batting 100%. PAH is a devastating, terminal, incurable disease.

I have a PAH support group which is a constant source of comfort and encouragement. Most importantly I am blessed with a loving, supportive husband who makes my life easier. He lifts my spirits when I'm down and serves as my nurse, friend, and my King. His unwavering support gives me the strength to face each day with hope and resilience.

Chapter Nine

"In my distress, I called to the Lord, and He answered me. (Psalm 120:1)

The afternoon was quiet, a rare moment of calm in my happening life. I had been napping, trying to catch up on rest, when I felt the gentle nudge of my Yorkie, Cody, and my Silky Terrier, Tiger. They were my constant companions, and their loyalty and love always brought me a sense of peace. They needed to go outside, so I groggily got up to let them out.

As I approached the stairs, a sudden wave of dizziness hit me. My vision blurred, and I felt myself losing consciousness. "Oh no!" I hollered out, but it was too late. I began to tumble down the stairs. The world became a chaotic blur of motion and pain. When I finally came to an abrupt stop at the bottom, I realized something was horribly wrong. My tibia had broken through the skin, and blood was pouring out onto the carpet. The pain was beyond anything I had ever experienced.

My husband had gone to church, leaving me alone at home. Panic set in as I saw the fire alarm on the adjacent wall. If I could just stand up and push the buttons, I could set off the alarm and alert my neighbors or the fire department. But when I tried to stand, my foot turned backward, and the pain forced me back down to the stairs. It felt like my foot was being torn off. The agony was indescribable.

Tiger started whining and needed to go to the bathroom. "I'm in a lot of pain; I can't let you out right now," I told him. He came over to me, started licking my toe, and then lay down beside me. Cody, my Yorkie, sat quietly at the top of the stairs, watching over us. I felt so helpless, sitting there with my dogs, watching the blood flow from my leg to the carpet.

I started screaming for help. "Somebody, please help me! Please!" But no one heard my cries. I knew if I could just hold on for one hour, my husband would be home. I had been there for half an hour, and the anxiety was overwhelming. "Help me, please help me. Lord, please help me!" I prayed desperately.

Suddenly, I heard a gentle voice in my head. It was calm and reassuring, telling me, "Turn around and crawl up the stairs." It made sense. By turning around and crawling, my ankle would be supported, and I might be able to make it back up.

Summoning all my strength, I turned around and slowly crawled up the stairs. Each movement sent waves of pain through my body, but I kept going, driven by the hope of reaching my bedroom and calling for help. When I finally reached my bedroom, a sense of relief washed over me. I had made it.

Overwhelmed with relief, I momentarily forgot my situation and tried to stand up again. As before, my foot twisted backward, and the pain returned with a vengeance. But then, something incredible happened. Just as God had promised that He would not put more on me than I could bear, I heard a sound like a loud lightning bolt, CRACK!, go off in my head. At that moment, all the pain vanished. It was as if a switch had been flipped in my brain, shutting off the pain centers.

My counselor later explained to me that this is a psychological phenomenon that cannot be easily explained. Some people have the ability to shut off the pain centers in their brains. But at that moment, I knew it was nothing I had done. It was a divine intervention. I gave all honor, praise, and glory to God.

With the pain gone, I was able to think clearly. I crawled to the other side of my bed, where my phone was on my nightstand. Lying on the floor, I called my husband. I wasn't thinking about anything else but him. So, he was the first call I made.

"Where are you?" I asked when he answered.

"I'm inside King Soopers buying food," he replied.

"Stop what you're doing and come home right away," I said, trying to keep my voice steady.

"What's going on?" he asked, concern creeping into his voice.

"Just come home right away," I insisted. He agreed and hung up.

A few minutes later, he called me back. "I'm on my way, but what's going on?"

"I fell down the stairs and broke my leg. My bone is sticking out, and I'm bleeding everywhere," I told him, finally letting the urgency and fear seep into my voice.

"Call 911! I'm coming as fast as I can," he said. He was just a few minutes away, but it felt like an eternity.

I hung up and dialed 911, explaining my situation. Before I could finish, my husband walked through the door. It was at that moment I could exhale. The ambulance arrived shortly after, following the blood trail up the stairs to my bedroom. They were amazed when I told them how I had crawled up the stairs, guided by the voice in my head.

The paramedics, along with my husband, picked me up and placed me on my bed. They began to pull my leg to straighten it and put it back in place. All I felt was tugging, but still no pain. They were amazed and kept telling me how strong I was, explaining how this procedure usually brought grown men to their knees. I told them that it wasn't my strength but God's. They gave me pain medication in the ambulance and took me to the hospital.

I remember waking up with a fixture on my leg to support the fracture. I kept it on for three days before going back into surgery to have a titanium rod placed in the shaft of my tibia to support the bone until it healed. The fibula, the smaller weight-bearing bone, was left to heal on its own. It healed incorrectly, presenting as a bulge on the side of my leg due to extra bone growth. However, the titanium rod is still in place to this day.

It takes eighteen months for bones to heal. I had to undergo intensive physical therapy, which was done from my home due to the pandemic. This was a blessing because I dislike physical therapy and probably wouldn't have gone otherwise. I do remember having some physical therapy at the hospital, but it didn't last very long.

Presently, I still have problems with my leg. It swells, which I'm told will probably never go away because of damaged blood and lymph vessels. Furthermore, the area where the bone came out is very sensitive to touch.

You might wonder why all these awful things keep happening to me. There was a time I asked the Lord the same question, "Lord, did you place me on this earth just to torture me?" I did want out; in fact, I tried. But you have to keep reading to find out about that. But first, another miracle.

Chapter Ten

"...I will never leave you nor forsake you." (Hebrews 13:5)

The second spinal stimulator that had been installed to manage the pain in my right leg initially worked fine. The battery pack was originally placed on my right hip, but a significant weight loss of 50 pounds meant it had to be relocated to the right side of my back. Despite my intense reluctance, I had to return to the same doctor who installed it. This was the doctor who once ignored my cries for help, leading to a massive saddle clot, and yet no other doctor would touch his work. It's an unwritten rule among medical professionals.

My husband and I visited this doctor over a span of four years. To my dismay, he didn't remember us. I tried to jog his memory about the past incident, and he apologized both for not remembering and for what had happened. His excuse was that he had seen hundreds of patients since then and couldn't possibly remember them all. I thought to myself, "But how many have you almost killed?"

He explained that installing spinal cord stimulators wasn't considered a "serious" surgery, so blood clot protocols weren't used. The incisions were superficial, he said. But someone forgot to tell my body that. Treating me like a human being instead of a drug addict would have prevented all of this. He assured me that blood clot protocol would be used in this surgery, and we agreed to proceed.

On the day of the surgery, I was extremely nervous. The nurses asked me multiple times about my allergies, and I repeatedly told them I was allergic to adhesive tape. They placed a red band around my wrist stating this fact and asked me again in the operating theater.

As the surgery time approached, my anxiety grew. I became tearful and began to shake. My husband was by my side, praying for me and assuring me that everything would be okay. But deep down, I had a gut feeling that something would go wrong. I didn't listen to my spirit. Big mistake. Huge mistake.

The nurses saw my anxiety and tried to comfort me, promising they would give me some calming medication soon. They reassured me that the doctor and staff would take care of me. My husband kissed me gently on the forehead, and they wheeled me into the operating theater.

The surgery went as planned. I had on compression socks, and all blood clot protocols were followed.

As soon as we got to the room, the drama started. The nurse said there were no orders for pain control. My husband exclaimed, "What do you mean you have no orders for pain control? She just had surgery!" The nurse explained there were no orders in the computer and that she would contact the doctor once he was out of surgery.

I had the pain medication from the surgery, so I was fine for the moment. It turned out the nurse had been looking in the wrong section of the computer. The doctor had indeed given me my own pain management team to ensure I was comfortable. The nurse's mistake was a false alarm, but the next issue wasn't.

I ate lunch around 1:00 PM. By 7:00 PM, my stomach began to swell as if I were six months pregnant, and I was in excruciating pain. I asked to see a doctor, but the nurse brushed it off, attributing it to my IBS. I hadn't eaten since 1:00 PM, so it couldn't be IBS. I knew my body, and my stomach wasn't this large when I arrived.

The nurse informed me that her shift was ending and she would inform the next nurse. For the next two hours, I was ignored. I got out of bed and began pacing, terrified and unsure of what was happening. I looked out the window at the Rocky Mountains, seeking solace. I cried out to the Lord for help.

My vital signs on the monitor began to alarm me. My blood pressure skyrocketed to 200/90, and my oxygen levels dropped to 83. The nurse rushed in, seeing my distress. "Mrs. Spicely, are you okay? Please get back in bed!" She said with panic in her eyes. I kept crying, unable to articulate my fear. As I returned to my bed to lay down, my muscles became rigid and I curled into a fetal position and couldn't talk.

The on-call doctor came in, insisting I was having a severe anxiety attack. "Mrs. Spicely, you are not passing a clot. I'm going to give you some medication to calm you down through your IV." The medication quickly reduced my anxiety.

Later that evening, my doctor came to see me. When I told him about my stomach, he curtly shrugged it off. "I performed the surgery. Everything went fine. I don't have anything to do with what's going on now," and he left. I never spoke to him again.

When I left the hospital, the incisions didn't feel right. A day later, they began itching. "Babe, something's not right," I told my husband. The sites were red with tiny blisters that began to weep. My husband confirmed there were staples, but the incisions were shiny. The shininess was surgical glue.

Despite telling them repeatedly about my adhesive allergy, the doctor closed my incisions with surgical glue. We went to the emergency room, where the doctor treated me for a severe allergic reaction to the glue now inside my body. I had to be on steroids and Benadryl for a while.

That night, around 2:00 AM, I woke up unable to breathe. My inhaler stopped the wheezing, but my chest was tight. Looking in the mirror, I saw my left eye drooping. I woke my husband, telling him I was having a stroke. My mouth drooped, and my left side went weak. The paramedics confirmed I was having a stroke.

At the hospital, tests ruled out a stroke and seizure. The neurologist diagnosed me with Functional Neurological Disorder (FND), caused by untreated PTSD. My brain had finally had enough, shutting down in a way that mimicked a stroke. I had no control over it, and the doctor's actions had triggered this disorder.

I stayed in the emergency room for 12 hours until the symptoms subsided. Since then, I've had 16 attacks.

A couple of days later, I woke up with my nightgown and bed soaked. Fluid was leaking from my back. When I bent over I felt a severe crippling pain in my back that almost brought me to my knees for two days, then subsided. On the third day, I spiked a high fever of 103°F. We went back to the emergency room, where they suspected an infection and warned me that the stimulator might need to come out. They said I might have to return to the same doctor. I refused.

The doctor stated he had a friend who was a neurosurgeon, and he would contact him to see if he would be willing to do the surgery. He further explained if he said no, I would have no other choice than to return to other neurosurgeon.

After what seemed like an eternity, the doctor returned with good news. His friend recognized my last name, and he turned out to be the neurosurgeon who had operated on my husband's back, so he agreed to do the surgery. We rejoiced in the goodness of the Lord. What are the chances that the ER Dr. in our neighborhood randomly calls his good friend, who just happens to be my husband's surgeon. All things are possible with God.

The fluid weeping from my body had picked up bacteria, leading to a staph infection. This wouldn't have happened if I hadn't been on steroids for the allergic reaction caused by the surgical glue. The steroids lowered my immune system making it easier for the bacteria to enter my body, causing the staph infection. I tried to sue the doctor, but no attorney would take my case. The damages weren't enough to cover the costs of bringing in experts to testify. This doctor is still out there, destroying lives.

Through it all, God has been my rock. He may not come when you want Him, but He is always on time.

Chapter Eleven

"But in my distress I cried out to the Lord; yes, I prayed to my God for help. He heard me from his sanctuary; my cry to him reached his ears…He reached down from heaven and rescued me; he drew me out of deep waters." (Psalm 18:6)

The hospital room was cold and sterile, the white walls and bright lights giving it an almost eerie atmosphere. I lay on the bed, trying to find some comfort despite the pain in my right hip. It had been months of agony, countless sleepless nights, and endless medication. The doctors had implanted a spinal stimulator to help control the pain, but now, due to a stubborn staph infection caused by the negligence of my doctor, it had to be removed. I felt a mix of dread and relief, knowing that another surgery was ahead but hoping it might finally bring some respite.

As I waited for the surgery, a new anesthesiologist came to speak with me. He had read through my medical records and noticed my history of anesthesia-induced nausea. His name was Dr. Williams, a kind-looking man with gentle eyes who seemed to understand my suffering. He asked if anyone had ever tried using propofol instead of the usual anesthesia.

"No," I replied, a bit wary. I knew about propofol but had never experienced it for surgery. Dr. Williams explained its properties, emphasizing how it could put me to sleep quickly and wake me up just as fast without the nauseating side effects I dreaded so much. His explanation was thorough, but I was already familiar with the drug. Still, I let him talk, appreciating his effort to ease my anxiety.

"But in my distress I cried out to the Lord; yes, I prayed to my God for help. He heard me from his sanctuary; my cry to him reached his ears…He reached down from heaven and rescued me; he drew me out of deep waters." (Psalm 18:6)

The hospital room was cold and sterile, the white walls and bright lights giving it an almost eerie atmosphere. I lay on the bed, trying to find some comfort despite the pain I was in. It had been months of agony, countless sleepless nights, and endless medication. The doctors had implanted a spinal stimulator to help control the pain, but now, due to a stubborn staph infection caused by the negligence of my doctor, it had to be removed. I felt a mix of dread and relief, knowing that another surgery was ahead but hoping it might finally bring some respite.

As I waited for the surgery, a new anesthesiologist came to speak with me. He had read through my medical records and noticed my history of anesthesia-induced nausea. His name was Dr. Williams, a kind-looking man with gentle eyes who seemed to understand my suffering. I began to question him about his experience with PAH patients. After all, my pulmonary Dr assured me he had requested a full PAH staff be in the operating room or at least a Cardiac Anesthetist. However, as I questioned him, the answer was no to both. He assured me he had worked with PAH patients before and he would take care of me.

He asked if anyone had ever tried using propofol instead of the usual anesthesia.

"No," I replied, a bit wary, because my mind was still perplexed about not having the proper staff in the operating theater for my PAH. I knew about propofol but had never experienced it for a major surgery. Dr. Williams explained its properties, emphasizing how it could put me to sleep quickly and wake me up just as fast without the nauseating side effects I dreaded so much. His explanation was thorough, but I was already familiar with the drug. Still, I let him talk, appreciating his effort to ease my anxiety.

"We'll try it on you," he suggested, his voice calm and reassuring. As my mind still pondered my situation, I blindly agreed, welcoming the thought of avoiding the sickness that usually followed my surgeries. Not thinking through the total ramifications of the decision Dr Williams had just made.

As the team prepped me for the procedure, I prayed silently. "Lord, please let this work. Please let this be the answer." My faith had carried me through many dark times, and I clung to it now, hoping for a miracle.

The surgery took about two hours. When they woke me up, the world around me was a blur of bright lights and muffled voices. But one thing was clear: the pain. It hit me like a tidal wave, crashing over every inch of my body. I screamed, my voice raw and desperate. "Put me back under! Put me back under! Please! Please!"

A nurse rushed to my side, her face pale and stricken. "Mrs. Spicely, we can't. It's too dangerous," she explained, her voice trembling with sympathy. I couldn't understand. The pain was unbearable, far worse than anything I had experienced before.

"Please, I'm in so much pain!" I continued to scream, my cries echoing in the sterile room. The nurse looked helpless, her eyes filled with regret.

Finally, another male nurse said, "Wait a minute, let me check something." He hurriedly pulled up my chart and scanned through the details. His eyes widened with realization. "You're on hydrocodone for pain control," He muttered to the other nurse, then turned to me. "That's why."

It turned out that my long-term use of opioids had created a high chemical level of hydrocodone in my brain. The medication they gave me during the surgery hadn't reached a level higher than the hydrocodone already in my system. Normally, anesthesia would have taken an hour or so before I woke up, giving the pain control enough time to rise above the hydrocodone levels. But with propofol, I woke up too quickly, and the pain medication hadn't had a chance to kick in.

The realization hit me hard. The anesthesiologist hadn't considered my opioid history before switching to propofol. I had undergone a procedure to clean up an infection and remove the spinal cord stimulator with no effective pain control.

As the nurses scrambled to figure out what to do, I cried out to the Lord. "Oh God, oh God, please help me!" My voice was filled with desperation and pain. In that moment of intense agony, something incredible happened. A sense of calm washed over me, a peace that I couldn't explain. It was as if God himself had reached down and wrapped me in His comforting embrace.

In the midst of my pain, He calmed my spirit and put me in a state of mind where I could think clearly. I realized that all my incisions were on my backside, and I was lying on my back. The solution was simple yet profound. I needed to sit up.

With a determination fueled by faith, I sat up on the edge of the bed. The nurses rushed back into the room, their faces a mix of shock and concern. "Mrs. Spicely, what are you doing? You can't go anywhere," one of them said, her voice filled with alarm.

"I'm not going anywhere. I'm just sitting on the edge of the bed," I replied, my voice steady despite the pain. I felt a strange sense of clarity, a calmness that allowed me to think rationally.

The nurse hesitated, then asked, "Do you want to sit in a chair?" I nodded, and she helped me move to a chair by the bedside. I took a deep breath, the pain still intense but more manageable now that I wasn't lying on my incisions.

"Go get me some ice! I demanded, my voice surprisingly strong. The nurse complied. She returned with a pack of ice, and I instructed her to pack my back with it. The cold sensation was a relief, numbing the pain just enough until the pain medication could take effect.

As I sat there, surrounded by the hum of hospital machines and the soft murmurs of the nurses, I felt an overwhelming sense of gratitude. God had given me the peace of mind to do what was necessary to stop the pain, just like a loving father guiding his child. He had shown up for me in my darkest moment, and I knew I wasn't alone.

Tears filled my eyes, but this time they weren't tears of pain. They were tears of thankfulness. "Thank you, Jesus," I whispered, feeling His presence beside me. The road to recovery was still ahead, but in that moment, I knew I had the strength to face it.

The hours passed slowly, but the pain medication finally started to work. The ice packs continued to provide relief, and the nurses, seeing that I was more comfortable, began to relax. They eventually moved me to my room where I would stay overnight.

As I sat by the window of my hospital room, watching the world outside, I felt a profound sense of peace. The journey had been painful, but it had also brought me closer to God. I knew that whatever challenges lay ahead, I could face them with faith and courage.

The experience had changed me. It taught me the power of prayer, the importance of faith, and the incredible strength that comes from trusting in the Lord. In my distress, I had cried out, and He had heard me yet again. He had reached down from heaven and rescued me, drawing me out of the deep waters of pain and despair.

I closed my eyes, took a deep breath, and whispered a prayer of gratitude. "Thank you, Jesus, for being with me every step of the way. Thank you for your love, your guidance, and your strength. I trust in you, now and always."

As I continued to heal, I knew that my journey wasn't over. There would be more challenges, more moments of pain and struggle. But I also knew that I wasn't alone. With God by my side, I had the strength to face whatever came my way.

And so, I embraced the future with hope and faith, knowing that I was held in the loving arms of my Savior. My cry had reached His ears, and He had answered. He had drawn me out of the deep waters and brought me to a place of peace and healing. For that, I would be forever grateful.

Chapter Twelve

In March of 2023, I found myself in the midst of a perfect storm. My life was filled with tumult, and everything seemed to be falling apart. I was at odds with my family, my PAH had taken a turn for the worse, and the medication I was on for depression was wreaking havoc on my liver, thyroid, and kidneys. After consulting with my doctors, we decided to taper off the Lithium and another antidepressant, Effexor that had long ceased to be effective. I was coping reasonably well until everything collapsed around me.

One day, while my husband and I were driving down I-70, one of Colorado's major highways, I received a call from a neighbor across the street from my mother. He told me he was looking through her front room window and saw her lying on the floor, unresponsive. My husband and I raced to her house, hearts pounding and tears streaming down our faces, crying out, "Oh God!" When we arrived, the scene was chaotic—police officers, ambulances, and fire trucks everywhere. Inside, my mother lay on the floor, looking more helpless than I had ever seen her. The memory still brings tears to my eyes. She kept saying, "Please cover me up. All these men in here." My mother, always a modest dresser, deserved her dignity, and I made sure they honored her request.

At 93, my mother was still able to take care of herself despite her dementia. That day marked a turning point for both of us. She had tripped and fallen when getting up to go to the bathroom, her legs tangled in the bedcovers. It was a Sunday, and her friend, who usually took her to church, couldn't reach her that morning. Concerned, the friend called a neighbor to check on her. My mother, finally untangling herself and trying to get up, shouted that she was okay. The neighbor, thinking she was fine, left. My mother, however, couldn't pull herself up and crawled to her living room, where she collapsed at the kitchen doorway. She lay there for two hours before the neighbor returned, at the behest of her friend's second call, still unable to reach my mom. He looked through the window, and saw her on the floor. That's when he contacted me.

They took my mother to a rehab center where she stayed for two weeks. When she returned home, it was clear she could no longer live alone. My brothers and I decided she would move to Atlanta with my second oldest brother. For the first time in my 60 years, I was not going to be around my mother. The impact of this separation was profound. Despite her verbal abuse, which she directed at everyone, I loved her dearly. She was my best friend. We talked about everything, laughed together, watched TV, and napped side by side. She cooked for me, and I confided my deepest thoughts to her. All of that was over. My heart broke.

In the span of three weeks, my mother was ripped from my life. During this time my health had declined, family drama escalated, adding to the immense stress. Combined with the tapering off of my depression medication, the emotional toll was overwhelming. I was hurting deeply and couldn't talk to my husband or mom about it. Although my husband was there for me, I needed my mother. The chemical transformations that were taking place in my brain made rational thinking out of my control.

I reached a breaking point and wanted the pain to end. I had made the decision to end my life five times before, but God had intervened each time. This time, I took my pain medication, put it in the glove compartment of my car, and drove aimlessly away from Denver, about an hour away. I stopped at a hotel, but forgot to retrieve the medication from the glove box. I checked in, grabbed something to eat, and went to my room. I called a few people, including my hairdresser, sending cryptic messages. She quickly realized I was saying goodbye. I also called my husband, who frantically tried to find out where I was. I wouldn't tell him. My son tried to reach me too, but I was too far gone. And then God stepped in.

Suddenly, I had severe chest pains, so intense I screamed in agony. It felt like God was saying, "You want to die? Here you go." Terrified, I called 911. The paramedics never figured out the cause of the pain and chalked it up to anxiety. However, I later found out they were wrong. I had pericarditis.

Shortly after, my husband developed a bad cold, and we tested him for COVID-19. The result was positive. Because I have PAH, they started him on medication immediately and advised him to isolate from me. We had already been in close contact, so I knew I was likely to get it. I bought several test kits and tested myself every day, each time negative, despite worsening symptoms.

I went to the emergency room because of breathing problems and chest pains, but the tests there also came back negative for COVID. Feeling worse, I called the ER again, asking to speak to a PAH doctor. PAH is a rare illness that many doctors are unfamiliar with, and the wrong medication can be fatal. The doctor on call, my former pulmonologist whom I had fired, responded with an attitude. He dismissed my concerns, suggesting I just had a bad cold and should do a nasal rinse and go to bed. He stated there was nothing he could do for me if I came to the ER. I angrily hung up the phone screaming, "This is why I fired you in the first place!"

The next morning, I ignored his advice and took another test—it was positive for COVID this time. I called my primary care physician, who urged me to come in immediately. Tests revealed I not only had COVID but also pericarditis, inflammation around the heart, explaining my severe chest pains. I had likely had COVID earlier without realizing it, and this was causing the chest pains I experienced in the hotel room. I left a curt message for the ER doctor to let him know the consequences of his dismissal of me. Of course he didn't respond.

Looking back, I can see God's hand in everything. I forgot to bring the pills into the hotel room. I was in too much pain to go back for them. Ignoring the doctor's advice and taking another test saved my life. COVID and PAH are a dangerous mix, and even a common cold can be serious. The doctor's willingness to dismiss me was the reason I had fired him in the pass.

Through all this, I've come to understand that all things work together for the good of those who love the Lord and are called according to His purpose.

Lessons from My Life

Listening Beyond the Words

As a parent, there are moments when our children teach us profound lessons. This realization dawned on me during a conversation with my son about his music preferences. Curious about why he exclusively listened to rap music, I asked him directly. His response was unexpected and eye-opening: "Mom, you have to listen to the story they are telling."

Intrigued by his perspective, I decided to listen. As he played his favorite tracks, I focused on the lyrics rather than the music itself. The stories I heard were heartbreaking—tales of children growing up in harsh environments, experiencing violence, losing loved ones, and making difficult choices just to survive. The pain in their words was palpable, flowing like an ocean relentlessly crashing against the shore. This experience shifted my understanding and appreciation for the music that resonated so deeply with my son.

My oldest son also has a passion for music. When he plays his face transforms with the intensity of each note as it vibrates through his body. He feels what he plays. It's a spiritual experience not just a musical instrument. That's what makes the difference. That's what has always made the difference even as a young child. I have a picture of him playing the drums while basking in the presence of the Holy Spirit. You can tell he is no longer in the church house but playing for God. I in turn get caught in his praise. Not just as a proud mom but also as praise and worshipper who can feel the presence of the Holy Spirit through gospel music. Tears fill my eyes and joy fills my heart. So proud yet so humble that God chose him for such a time as this.

Reflecting on this lesson, I realized how similar their approach to music was to my own approach when talking to people in pain. I look beyond their immediate expressions of suffering to understand the deeper story their spirit is telling. My son's way of connecting with the world through rap music was his method of empathy, similar to how I connect with others through conversations and support. My other son's connection to music and how it ushers him into God's presence is how I survive my trials and tribulations.

This insight made me consider how I process music myself. When I was younger, slow songs were my refuge, especially during difficult times. I would lie on the floor next to the stereo, letting the music wash over me, feeling understood and less alone in my pain. Slow music, particularly gospel songs, still captivates my soul, lifting my spirit above my circumstances and bringing me peace and comfort through my faith in God.

This led me to a broader question: What are we not listening to in our own lives? Are we missing the cries for help from our children, hidden in their music or behavior? Are we too caught up in our own emotions—anger, disappointment, or defeat—to truly hear the stories behind their actions?

One poignant example of this came from my time as a Medical Assistant Instructor at a technical college. I loved my job, which combined education with entertainment to engage students. I often used humor and real-life scenarios to teach, creating a vibrant and dynamic classroom environment.

However, a tragic incident with a bright, cheerful student who hid her pain behind a smile changed everything. Despite her outward cheerfulness, she was struggling with deep depression following her boyfriend's suicide. I became her support, calling her when she missed classes and encouraging her to succeed. Yet, one day, she disappeared, and a few days later, her friends informed me she had taken her own life.

The news devastated me. I questioned everything I had done or failed to do. Could I have prevented her death by listening more closely, by taking different actions? The guilt and sorrow were overwhelming. This tragedy taught me a painful but vital lesson: We must always listen deeply to those around us, especially those who seem to be hiding their pain behind a smile.

In the wake of her death, I realized the importance of giving a voice to my own depression. Despite the stigma, I spoke openly about my struggles, ensuring others knew they were not alone. This commitment to transparency and support became a cornerstone of my life and work.

The lessons from my son and my student reinforced a crucial truth: We must listen beyond the surface, to the stories hidden within the words and actions of those around us. Whether it's the music our children listen to, the behavior of our students, or the quiet cries of those in pain, we need to hear the deeper stories. By doing so, we can offer the understanding, support, and love that can make a profound difference in their lives and our own.

Remember, no matter how difficult life gets, **YOU ARE NOT ALONE**. Listen to the stories around you, and let your own story be heard.

Depression: The Other Silent Killer

On August 11, 2014, the world was shocked by the news that Robin Williams, the beloved actor and comedian, had taken his own life at the age of 63. Reports indicated that Mr. Williams had been battling depression for a long time. We later found out that his illness, Lewy Body Dementia likely had a lot to do with his decision. Though I didn't know him personally, his struggle resonated deeply with me because I am familiar with the dark corridors of depression.

Depression is often misunderstood, and well-meaning but ignorant (lacking knowledge) comments can exacerbate the suffering. People have said things like, "Just get over it; yesterday is gone," or, "You lack faith in the Lord," and even, "You're a very selfish person." Do you think someone wants to be depressed, shunned by friends, co-workers, and even family? Here's another one: "She just wants attention." Well, yes, when someone feels like ending their life, they are indeed crying out for help. Wouldn't you?

Comments like these can be harmful, akin to a mild form of bullying, pushing someone further into despair. When a person already feels worthless, these attitudes reinforce their feelings of isolation and hopelessness. Sometimes, depression can strike without an apparent cause. I woke up every morning feeling depressed without any trigger, and even though getting out of the house can help, the feeling often returns.

Judging what you don't understand can be incredibly damaging. Depression can affect anyone—you, your child, parent, or friend. We are not crazy attention-seekers but individuals dealing with deep-seated issues that need to be addressed. Society often forces people to hide their depression, but speaking out is crucial for healing.

When I stepped forward about my depression, I faced significant judgment, but I never stopped talking about it. People began sharing their stories with me—how they used drugs to mask their pain until they found proper treatment for their depression.

I understand the desperation that comes with depression. I once drank a whole bottle of vodka, despite not being a drinker, and paid dearly for it. After being diagnosed with a neurological disorder, I attempted suicide five times. The combined weight of chronic pain and depression felt unbearable.

Eventually, I found help through medication and therapy. The SSRIs (Selective Serotonin Reuptake Inhibitors) I was prescribed temporarily changed my life. They balanced my brain chemistry, allowing me to experience "normal" emotions without the constant cloud of depression. I could cry and then move on, instead of being paralyzed by my emotions for months. I was misconstrued as advocating medication as the only treatment for depression. That was never my stance. Medication was the right treatment for me at that time in my life.

If you take away anything from my story, let it be this: Do not judge what you do not understand. Depression is a complex and often invisible illness. The brain is an organ like the liver, pancreas, and stomach to name a few. They all fail at times. The brain is no different just because it has a spiritual component. Don't let someone tell you otherwise. Also take note that depression can also manifest in the stomach instead of the brain causing symptoms such as nausea, bloating, diarrhea, constipation, cramps, and ulcers.

To my fellow sufferers, remember—you are not alone. There is help, and there is hope. Speaking out and seeking help can lead to a better, more manageable life. If you need emergent help go to your nearest emergency room. Understanding and compassion from others can make all the difference.

Don't try to stand on faith that you don't have. Seek help. It may cost your life.

I was eventually cured by the hand of God, but it was on his timing at 60 years old. I no longer take any anti-depressants. Why? Because He had a plan. It wasn't about me. It was about others who suffered around me. I was/am their voice. I spoke up to teach about it and against those who tried to shame me due to their lack of understanding. My speaking to someone who I saw hurting actually thwarted a suicide attempt that I didn't know was about to happen. Like kind recognizes pain and anguish.

Milton Keynes UK
Ingram Content Group UK Ltd.
UKHW020926030824
446369UK00005B/18